Mapping Global Issues

Endangered Species

Mapping Global Issues

Endangered Species

Peter Littlewood

A+

Smart Apple Media

Published in the United States by Smart Apple Media
PO Box 3263, Mankato, Minnesota 56002

Series concept: Alex Woolf   Editor and picture researcher: Alex Woolf
Designer: Jane Hawkins   Map illustrator: Stefan Chabluk

Library of Congress Cataloging-in-Publication Data

Littlewood, Peter.
Endangered species / Peter Littlewood.
p. cm.—(Mapping global issues)
Includes index.
Summary: "Using maps and charts, describes the species of animals that are endangered, why they are threatened, and what can be done to stop the decline of their species"—Provided by publisher.
ISBN 978-1-59920-507-6 (library binding)
1. Endangered species—Juvenile literature. I. Title.
QH75.L575 2012
333.95'22—dc23
                              2011017064

Picture credits
Corbis: 10 (Atlantide Phototravel), 30 (Michael & Patricia Fogden), 42–43 (Dan Guravich).
Jutzi, Michael: 31.
Nature Picture Library: 35 (David Fleetham), 39 (Nick Gordon).
Science Photo Library: 7 (Mark Garlick).
Shutterstock: 19 (Uryadnikov Sergey), 21 (Mike Flippo), 22 (FloridaStock), 27 (Arkady Mazor), 41 (Eric Gevaert).

Cover picture: The orangutan is a critically endangered species of primate that lives on the islands of Borneo and Sumatra.

Every attempt has been made to clear copyright. Should there be any inadvertent omission, please apply to the publisher for rectification.

Map sources
9 (Artificial Habitat), 13 (www.seaworld.org), 15 (Save the Tiger Fund), 17 (based on William Temple Hornaday's late-ninteenth-century research), 25 (U.S. Geological Survey), 29 (WWF), 33 (Florida Museum of Natural History), 37 (National Oceanic and Atmospheric Administration).

Printed at CT, China
SL001632US

PO1035
08-2011

9 8 7 6 5 4 3 2 1

Contents

A Brief History of Extinction

Death is the one certainty in life. And one day, in the very distant future, the last human on Earth will die. That is, of course, if we don't destroy ourselves much sooner through our own actions. Extinction—the total dying out of a species of plant or animal—can be a natural process. Climate changes over time may create conditions that a species cannot survive. Perhaps a new, better-adapted, and more successful species gradually evolves and pushes aside an older one. Sometimes, a particular species is just too tasty and can't run very fast!

CASE STUDY

A PLANETARY WHODUNNIT!

About 65 million years ago, at the end of the Cretaceous period, something happened on Earth that destroyed an entire species of animal life: the dinosaurs. All of the dinosaurs disappeared from the fossil record during a period of approximately a million years or less after dominating the planet for the previous 165 million years. What could have caused this catastrophic extinction? There are several possible answers:

• The volcano theory proposes that a large increase in volcanic eruptions threw enormous quantities of ash and poisonous gases into the atmosphere, suffocating the dinosaurs.

• The impact theory suggests that Earth was hit by a massive asteroid, perhaps 6.2 miles (10 km) wide. Clay rich in the mineral iridium, which is rare on Earth but often present in meteorites, is found across the world in the rock strata (layers) from the late Cretaceous period, supporting this theory. The impact of a huge asteroid would have sent enormous clouds of dust and ash into the atmosphere causing rapid global cooling and darkness. This would have killed many plants and, in turn, caused plant-eating dinosaurs to starve to death.

• Another theory is that a disease—a kind of dinosaur plague—killed all the dinosaurs.

An asteroid some 6 miles (10 km) across may have hit Earth's oceans 65 million years ago. Water vapor thrown into the atmosphere by the impact would have lowered global temperatures and perhaps caused the extinction of the dinosaurs.

The Human Threat

One species has grown in numbers at an alarming rate, causing many others to become endangered or extinct. It has robbed other plants and animals of their habitats (the environment that is favorable to their species), hunted or harvested them to extinction, and caused pollution that has endangered or killed off other, more sensitive species. It has even altered the planet's climate. The destructive species is *Homo sapiens sapiens*. It's us, the people of the world. In the last few centuries alone, we have pushed hundreds, if not thousands, of species to extinction and have endangered thousands more.

Prehistoric Extinction

Modern humans, with all of our technological advances, are much more threatening to other species than we used to be. Looking back at our ancestors, we can see that our destructive habits have a very long history.

The woolly mammoth is one example. According to the fossil record, these animals first appeared across what is now Europe and Asia about 300,000 years ago. At that time, the world was in the grip of an ice age. The climate was generally much colder than it is today. The mammoths, with their thick, woolly coats, were well adapted to living in the icy conditions of the time. These herbivores ate grasses, plants, and twigs.

Mammoths thrived for about 280,000 years, reaching a peak in population about 42,000 years ago, when glacier coverage was at its greatest. As the planet gradually warmed up, their numbers began to decline. About 6,000 years ago, their habitat had shrunk to just 10 percent of what it had been at its peak. But it was humans who sealed the mammoths' fate. The extreme cold of the mammoths' chosen territories had prevented contact with humans, but as temperatures increased, humans began hunting them. Scientists believe the last mammoth died about 5,000 years ago.

Death of the Dodo

The dodo was a bird that lived on Mauritius, an island in the Indian Ocean, off the coast of Africa. Portuguese sailors discovered the island in 1598. If they hadn't, the dodo may still be alive today. From descriptions and illustrations of the time, we know that the dodo was a gray, turkey-sized bird with a big beak and a fluffy white plume of tail feathers. It had small stubby wings, useless for flying—but it didn't need to fly, as it had no predators.

When the sailors landed on the island, they were amazed that these birds were not frightened and didn't try to run away as humans walked up to them. The sailors named them "dodo," which means stupid in Portuguese! Dodos didn't realize that humans were dangerous, so the sailors found them very easy to kill for food. The dodos made their nests on the ground. Dodo eggs and chicks were trampled on and eaten by the rats, pigs, and monkeys that had been transported on the ships. Within a few years of their discovery, very few dodos were left. By 1681, the species was extinct.

PERSPECTIVES

KILLER INSTINCT

When the sailors first landed in Mauritius and saw the gentle dodos, it never occurred to them to do anything other than to club them to death . . . Presumably, hitting defenceless [defenseless], tame, flightless birds over the head with a club was just something to do.

Richard Dawkins, *The God Delusion*, 2006

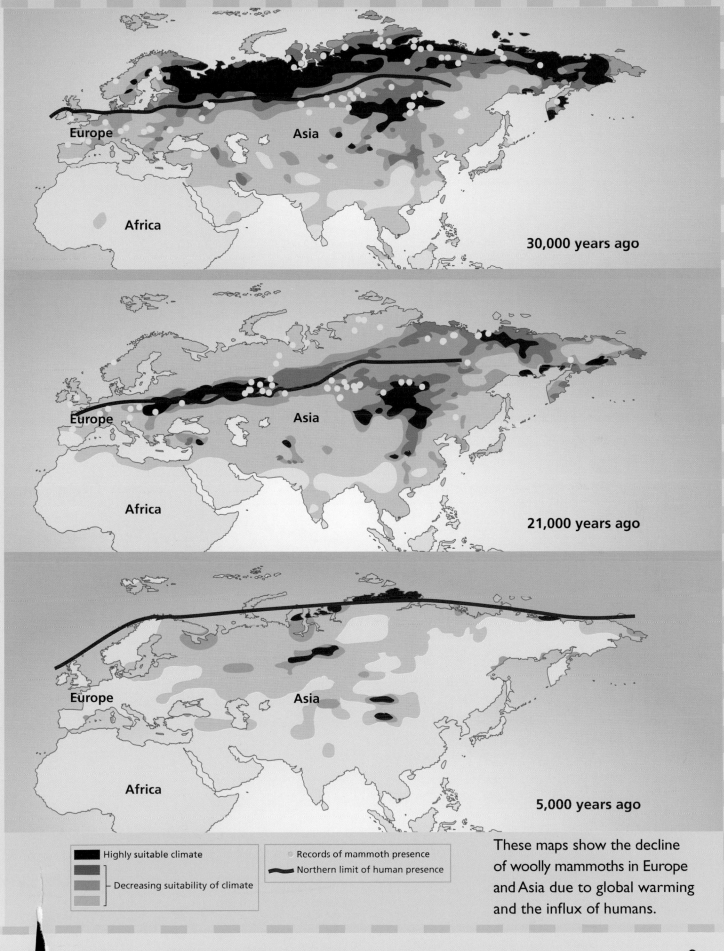

Europe

Asia

Africa

30,000 years ago

Europe

Asia

Africa

21,000 years ago

Europe

Asia

Africa

5,000 years ago

■ Highly suitable climate

⬛ ⬛ ⬛ ⬛ Decreasing suitability of climate

○ Records of mammoth presence

━ Northern limit of human presence

These maps show the decline of woolly mammoths in Europe and Asia due to global warming and the influx of humans.

9

This monk in Thailand is helping to care for a tiger that has been injured by poachers at Wat Pa Luangta Bua, the "Tiger Temple."

Monitoring Endangered Species

An endangered species is one in which the number of remaining animals has become so low that it is in danger of extinction. A species becomes "extinct in the wild" when it has not been seen in the wild for at least 50 years. It can be classified as fully extinct only after the last captive member of the species has died.

With all our technological advances, modern humans destroy more species than our ancestors, but we are also better at knowing we're doing it. We have become skilled at monitoring the world's species. This has allowed conservation groups to try to protect species when they become endangered. Hopefully, this will prevent more species from becoming extinct.

The Red List

The International Union for the Conservation of Nature (IUCN) publishes the Red List of endangered species. The list is based on the evidence of more than 1,700 scientists working in 130 countries around the world. Their job is to protect and learn more about rare species. According to the Red List, some 17,300 species of the nearly 56,000 species assessed so far are considered under threat. This includes 12 percent of the world's birds, 21 percent of mammals, 30 percent of reptiles, 31 percent of amphibians, 37 percent of fish, and 70 percent of the world's plants.

Extinction Rates

It is likely that the Red List massively underestimates the extent of the problem because it takes a long time to gather data on each species. The gap between official statistics and reality can be seen when one looks at extinction data. As of March 2010, 869 extinctions had been officially recorded since 1500 BC. A further 208 species are listed as possibly extinct, meaning that they have not been seen for decades. However, the IUCN has calculated that between 100

and 1,000 of every million species on the planet become extinct each year.

Fossil records show that the background rate of extinction (the rate at which it would occur naturally without human interference) is around one in every million species per year. Alarmingly, the rate of extinction that humans cause is similar to that experienced by the dinosaurs. That means we're as effective at wiping out species as the giant asteroid or dinosaur plague that occurred 65 million years ago!

FACTS and FIGURES

TEEMING WITH LIFE AND DEATH

There are 1.8 million known and scientifically named species on Earth. Only about 56,000 of these have been assessed by the IUCN's panel of scientists. However, it is believed that there could be as many as 30 million species in existence on Earth. And this is only about 3 percent of all species ever to have lived on Earth.

Source: IUCN

The current rate of extinctions is at least 100 times the background rate, but some estimates suggest it is as much as as 10,000 times the background rate! If present rates continue, half of all species on Earth could be extinct by 2100.

Edward O. Wilson, Harvard biologist, 2007

Hunting and Poaching

Unlike our mammoth-hunting ancestors, most people today get their food from farms. So why does hunting continue? Hunters argue that they help maintain healthy populations of wild animals, and a skillful hunter can ensure the kill is swift. The Inuit hunt seals for food and clothing. They claim they hunt humanely and do not endanger the seal population. The problem is that not all hunters behave responsibly. Animals sometimes endure lingering, painful deaths, and hunting has brought some species to the brink of extinction.

Gorillas

Gorillas, our closest relatives after the chimpanzees, are on the edge of extinction. As of February 2010, there were only about 780 mountain gorillas left in the wild. They live in two regions in Central Africa, just 28 miles (45 km) apart. They live in the Bwindi Impenetrable National Park in Uganda and the mountainous Virungas region, which straddles the borders of Rwanda and the Democratic Republic of Congo (DRC).

The situation is slightly better for western lowland gorillas, but they are still classified on the Red List as critically endangered. Their population has decreased by 80 percent in just three generations. Currently, there are thought to be approximately 100,000 to 125,000 of the lowland gorillas left in the wild and spread across a huge territory. Their dense and often impenetrable forest habitat makes it difficult to calculate their true numbers.

The Gorilla Meat Trade

Gorillas have become endangered because they are hunted for their meat. In the DRC, cattle and chicken meat is not plentiful and is too expensive for many people. It makes economic sense for people to venture deep into the rain forest and hunt gorillas. The prices they obtain for gorilla meat make it worthwhile. A hand-sized piece of precut and smoked gorilla meat sells for about five times the price of beef. Customers can also buy gorilla hands for about $6 each. These are considered a delicacy.

CLOSE RELATION

No one who looks into a gorilla's eyes—intelligent, gentle, vulnerable—can remain unchanged, for the gap between ape and human vanishes; we know that the gorilla still lives within us.

George B. Schaller, in *National Geographic*, October 1995

An undercover investigation, conducted by the conservation group Endangered Species International (ESI), took place in the Kouilou region of the DRC in 2009. It found that at least two gorillas per week, out of a population of about 200, are being killed and sold as wild game meat. That means 50 percent of the population is being killed in one year. At that rate, gorillas could be extinct in the region in less than 10 years.

This is the story in just one area of the DRC, but it is likely that gorillas are being killed at similar rates across many parts of their range. Gorillas receive very little protection. Although there are laws in place to protect them from hunters, little is done to enforce these laws, so the hunting continues.

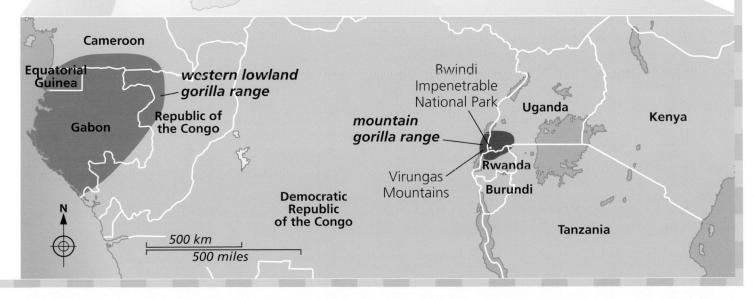

This map shows the ranges of the western lowland and mountain gorillas.

Cameroon

Equatorial Guinea

western lowland gorilla range

Gabon

Republic of the Congo

Bwindi Impenetrable National Park

Uganda

Kenya

mountain gorilla range

Rwanda

Virungas Mountains

Burundi

Democratic Republic of the Congo

N

500 km
500 miles

Tanzania

For now, the gorillas are protected to some extent by the remoteness of their habitats. Yet people are encroaching ever deeper into the forests, looking for food and firewood.

The Ivory Trade

The African elephant is so threatened by poaching that it could be extinct in just 15 years. In 2009, the elephant population was 600,000, but this has been decreasing by 38,000 each year. Many more elephants die each year than are born. This is in spite of an international ban on the trade of ivory (the substance elephants' tusks are made of) in force since 1990.

Ivory is used to make many kinds of ornaments and jewelry and is highly valued in East Asia. Although it is illegal to buy and sell ivory products, the trade is growing. In 2010, 35 ounces (1 kg) of ivory was worth about $6,200. As a pair of male elephant tusks may weigh more than 440 pounds (200 kg), it is easy to see how money can be made by poaching elephants.

PERSPECTIVES

DESPERATE MEASURES

Many African countries are suffering terrible drought and local people are desperate. Killing elephants brings money, alas.

Heather Sohl, World Wildlife Fund (WWF)

The trade continues almost unchecked throughout Central and West Africa. For example, Zakouma National Park in Chad had 3,885 elephants in 2005. By 2009, there were only 617. In the same time period, 11 rangers (people whose job it is to protect the elephants) were shot by poachers. Only the tusks are taken by the poachers. The rest of the elephant is left to rot where it falls.

Tigers in Danger

In 2010, according to the World Wildlife Fund (WWF), there were just 3,200 to 3,500 tigers left in the wild—that is the total number worldwide! In 1900, there were more than 100,000 tigers. The main reasons for their decline are:

- coming into conflict with humans and livestock and consequently being killed,
- losing their habitat, and
- being targeted by hunters for the illegal trade of tiger parts.

Tiger Pills

In Chinese medicine, tiger parts are thought to have health-giving properties. The medicines are of questionable value: tiger whiskers are supposed to cure toothaches; a tiger's nose, if hung over a marriage bed, is said to increase the chances of having a boy; and tiger bone wine (worth $240 for 17 ounces (500 mL) is said to cure arthritis and rheumatism.

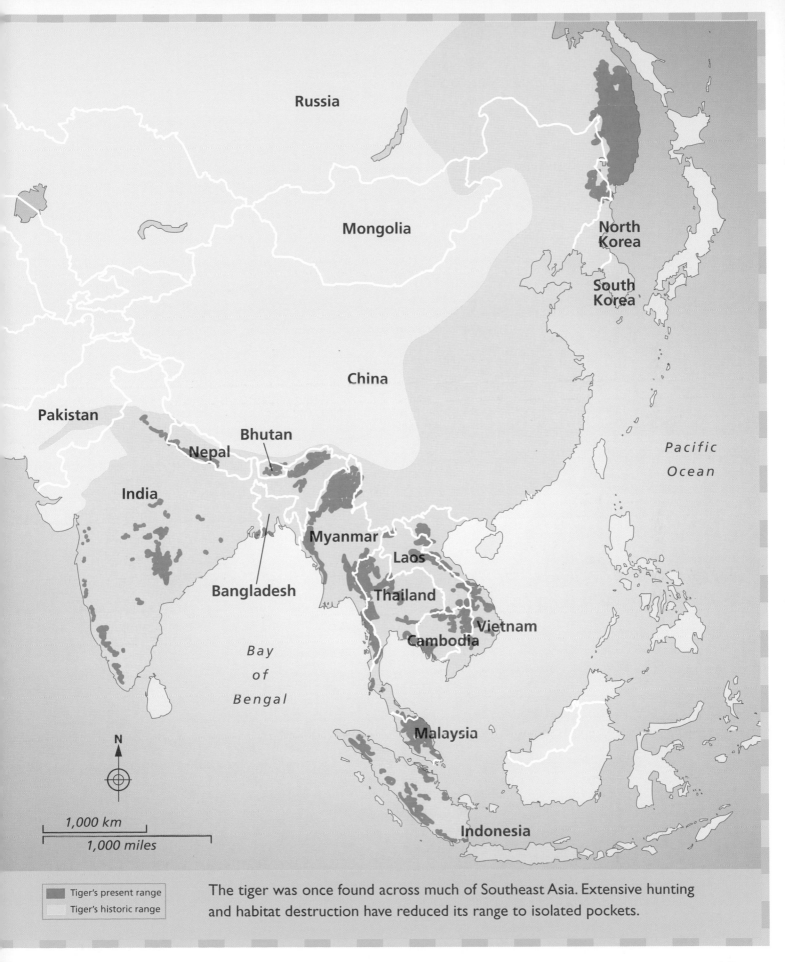

Russia

Mongolia

China

North Korea

South Korea

Pacific Ocean

Pakistan

Nepal

Bhutan

India

Bangladesh

Myanmar

Laos

Thailand

Vietnam

Cambodia

Bay of Bengal

N

1,000 km

1,000 miles

Malaysia

Indonesia

Tiger's present range
Tiger's historic range

The tiger was once found across much of Southeast Asia. Extensive hunting and habitat destruction have reduced its range to isolated pockets.

A single wild tiger, sold on the black market, can be worth up to $50,000. It is easy to see how a poor farmer, expecting to make just a few hundred dollars a year to feed himself and his family, is likely to be tempted by the rewards of hunting a tiger.

Buffalo

The Bering Strait is a narrow waterway between Asia and North America, but scientists believe there was a land bridge at one time that connected Asia and North America. It is believed that during the last ice age, wild buffalo crossed the land bridge to North America. The buffalo migrated to what we know as the prairies of Canada and the United States.

PERSPECTIVES

RUTHLESS SLAUGHTER

Thirty years ago millions of the great unwieldy animals existed on this continent. Innumerable droves roamed, comparatively undisturbed and unmolested . . . Many thousands have been ruthlessly and shamefully slain every season for the past twenty years or more by white hunters and tourists merely for their robes, and in sheer wanton sport, and their huge carcasses left to fester and rot, and their bleached skeletons to strew the deserts and lonely plains.

"In the Prime of the Buffalo" by J. F. Baltimore.
The Overland Monthly & Out West Magazine,
November 1889

In the 1600s, an estimated 50 million to 60 million buffalo (or North American bison) roamed the plains of North America. They were hunted by Native Americans for centuries, but this had little impact on such an enormous population. The Native Americans used almost all parts of the buffalo they killed. The meat was eaten. Hides were made into moccasins, leggings, other clothing, teepee covers, and carrying cases. Fur was woven into ropes or used for stuffing. Hooves were boiled to make glue, and horns were used to make arrow points, ladles, spoons, and cups. Even buffalo dung was utilized as fuel or as a stone polish.

In the 1800s, settlers saw the value of the buffalo as a source of food, clothing, and raw materials. A high-quality buffalo hide was worth $50 and an average one was worth $3—at a time when a laborer's wages were about $1 a day. Mass hunting, with the use of powerful hunting rifles, reduced buffalo numbers at an alarming rate. The hunters used the buffalo hides for leather or to make thick winter coats. They also took the buffalo tongues, which were considered a delicacy. The carcasses were left to rot on the plains. When all that remained were the bones, these were gathered up and shipped via rail for processing into fertilizer.

Back from the Brink

By 1890, there were probably fewer than 2,000 buffalo left in North America. By this time, when it was almost too late,

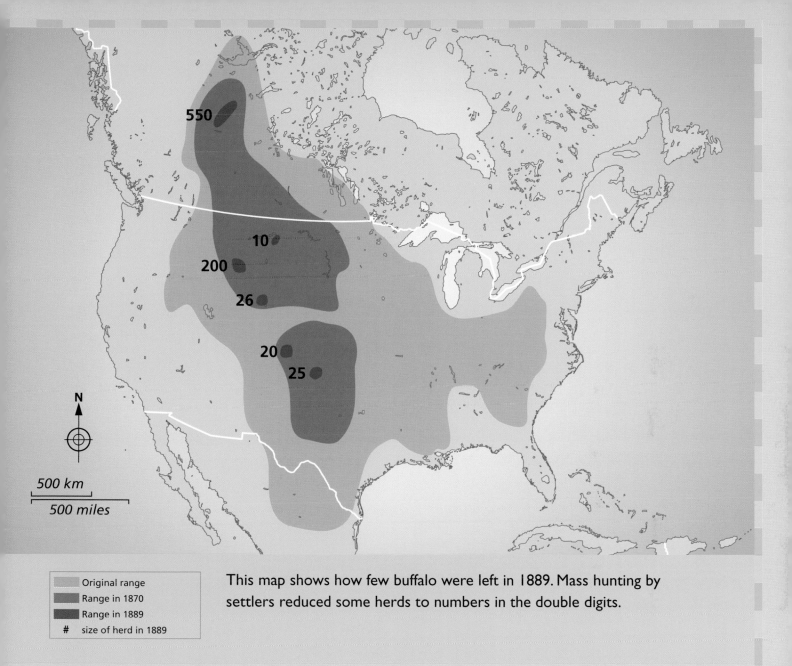

This map shows how few buffalo were left in 1889. Mass hunting by settlers reduced some herds to numbers in the double digits.

Original range
Range in 1870
Range in 1889
\# size of herd in 1889

people realized that the buffalo needed protecting if it was to survive. With careful conservation and captive breeding, there are now approximately 500,000 buffalo in North America, living on about 4,000 privately owned ranches. The animals are bred for their meat, which is low in fat and high in protein, making it a good choice for those who are health conscious. There are very few truly wild buffalo in North America. The Red List estimates that just 15,000 wild buffalo roam across the continent.

In the case of the buffalo, humans realized what they were doing just in time. This should give us some cause for hope. If the buffalo can be brought back from the brink of extinction, we may be able to save other species in the same way.

Habitat Loss, Pollution, and Invaders

As one of the most adaptable species on the planet, humans are able to survive in all kinds of conditions—from the frozen wasteland of the Arctic to the dry heat of the Sahara. We do this by making things to help us, such as thermal clothing and sun block, but also by changing the landscape to suit our purposes: clearing forests for timber and farmland, for example. Unfortunately, in making these changes, we often endanger animal and plant species that depend on these habitats for survival.

Change

The majority of animal and plant species are far less adaptable than humans. They have evolved over millions of years in a particular environment and are adapted to those conditions. When the conditions change, they struggle to survive. This often causes a chain reaction. If one creature dies out, so do the predators that depend on it for their survival, and so on up the food chain. And it's not just changes to the landscape that can threaten the animals and plants of a particular habitat. Other human-caused threats include pollution and the introduction of new species.

Man of the Forest

The orangutan is one of our closest relatives, sharing 96.4 percent of our DNA. Its name means "man of the forest" in the Malay language. Orangutans used to live across a huge area of Southeast Asian rain forest, stretching from southern China to the foothills of the Himalayas and south to Java. Today, they survive only on the Indonesian islands of Borneo and Sumatra.

FACTS and FIGURES

DECLINE DUE TO DEFORESTATION

A century ago, the combined orangutan population of Borneo and Sumatra was around 230,000. In 2010, orangutans on the two islands numbered no more than 62,500. In the last 10 years alone, their numbers have fallen by up to 50 percent. It's easy to see why. In just 20 years, between 1990 and 2010, about 80 percent of suitable habitat has been destroyed. Of the remaining forest, only 2 percent is properly protected.

Source: WWF UK, 2010

Tragically, this species of orangutan is now under threat of extinction and could disappear from Borneo's wild forests by 2020.

The IUCN Red List of 2010 classifies Bornean orangutans as endangered and Sumatran orangutans as critically endangered. The main threats to the orangutan's survival come from commercial logging (much of which is illegal) and land clearance for agriculture and the creation of plantations. A 2007 United Nations Environment Programme report suggested that 98 percent of Indonesia's rain forests may be destroyed by 2022. If this happens, it would mean the end of the orangutan.

Here Today, Gone Tomorrow?

The Bornean clouded leopard is a medium-sized wild cat that shares the orangutan's home in the rain forests of Borneo and Sumatra. In 2007, it was discovered to be a separate species from the clouded leopard that lives in mainland China. Despite its name, it is not a leopard, but a type of wild cat. Its name comes from the oval-shaped markings on its coat, which are said to resemble clouds.

The Bornean clouded leopard weighs up to 55 pounds (25 kg) and uses its agility to hunt at ground level. Its canine teeth are up to 2 inches (5 cm) long—longer than those of any other big cat and only exceeded relative to its body size by the saber-tooth tiger of prehistoric times. As Bornean clouded leopards live deep in the rain forests and are habitually secretive, it is very difficult to determine how many are left. According to the most optimistic estimates, there are 11,000 of these wild cats in Borneo and 7,000 in Sumatra.

CASE STUDY

SHOULD WE PANDER TO THE PANDA?

The giant panda, which lives in the mountains of Sichuan, Shaanxi, and Gansu provinces of central China, is recognized worldwide as a symbol for conservation. It is regarded by the IUCN as a "conservation-reliant endangered species," meaning that it is dependent on human efforts for its survival. There are certainly no more than 3,000 left in the wild. Most of these live in 40 reserves in central China.

During the late 1940s, China's rapidly expanding population caused a growing demand for land and raw materials. As a result, much of the panda's habitat—mountainous forests with thick stands of bamboo—was destroyed. The panda was also hunted for its fur. In the 1950s, when people realized pandas were in danger of dying out, they often caged pandas to preserve them. But caged pandas failed to reproduce, further endangering the species.

Some conservationists now consider the giant panda to be beyond help. Certainly, it is a species on which a great deal of money has been spent over the last few decades with little effect. Some believe that it would now be better to let the giant panda fend for itself.

A giant panda feeds on bamboo in its mountainous forest home. This iconic symbol for the conservation movement is able to survive only due to human intervention.

The bald eagle, the national symbol of the United States, was driven to the brink of extinction by farmers' use of DDT as a pesticide.

A Twin Threat

Like the orangutans, the Bornean clouded leopard is threatened by habitat destruction. And, despite being a protected species, it is hunted for its pelt (skin), and other parts. The bones and teeth of Bornean clouded leopards are thought to have healing properties in Chinese medicine. Threatened by hunters and habitat destruction, this wild cat could be extinct in the wild by 2022— along with the orangutan. If that happens, the Bornean clouded leopard would have disappeared just 15 years after humans realized it existed as a distinct species.

Pollution

Animals become endangered for many reasons. Hunting and habitat destruction are highly visible causes. Pollution from factory waste and agriculture is equally destructive. The bumblebee bat of Thailand and Myanmar—the world's smallest mammal—is threatened by pollution from cement factories in Myanmar.

DDT and Birds of Prey

Sometimes, people have used chemicals on the land without realizing the consequences. In the 1950s, a chemical called DDT was introduced to farming. A pesticide, it was highly effective in controlling insect pests. No one was aware of its bioaccumulative effects. In other words, the chemical became concentrated in the fatty tissues of many species of animals that were exposed to it.

DDT made its way into the waterways, affecting the zooplankton, tiny creatures that are present in open water. Fish would eat the zooplankton, accumulating DDT in their bodies. Birds of prey, such as the osprey, ate the fish, which gave them large doses of DDT. On land, DDT found its way into worms and bugs, which were eaten by small birds such as robins. In turn, these were eaten by birds of prey such as eagles.

The DDT did not kill the birds of prey, but it affected the way their bodies metabolized calcium. As a result, their eggs had thinner, weaker shells, which collapsed under the adult bird while it sat on the eggs in the nest. The use of DDT brought many species of bird of prey to the brink of extinction in the United States. For example, there were thought to be as many as 500,000 bald eagles in the United States in the 1700s. By the mid-1950s, there were only 412 breeding pairs in the whole country. The use of DDT was banned in the United States in 1972. Bird of prey numbers have recovered as a result.

PERSPECTIVES

PUT AWAY THAT DDT

Hey farmer, farmer,

Put away that DDT now

Give spots on my apples

But leave me the birds and the bees

Please!

Joni Mitchell from the song
"Big Yellow Taxi"

Otters

European otters are beautiful, secretive creatures—graceful swimmers and lethal hunters. At one time, they were plentiful in the rivers in the United Kingdom, but by the 1970s they had almost disappeared. This was due to the pollution of Britain's waterways by chemicals used in the manufacture of pesticides and electrical equipment. The chemicals bioaccumulated and affected the otter's ability to reproduce. The species almost became extinct across much of its range.

Since 1993, when an initiative was launched to clean up the rivers in the United Kingdom, the otter has returned. Legislation banning or restricting the use of damaging chemicals across much of Europe has, according to conservationists, led to the otter's gradual recovery. However, the IUCN still classifies it as "near threatened."

Alien Invaders

In the case of pollution, we have seen how human actions can have unintended consequences for plants and animals. People have also introduced a species to a country or region where it had not existed before.

This occurred with the rhododendron, a shrub-like plant that grows naturally in the Himalayas. It was introduced into the United Kingdom in the 1700s. By Victorian times, it was a popular garden plant. However, there is almost nothing in the United Kingdom that eats rhododendron, and the plant is capable of spreading rapidly. It shades the ground beneath it, making it impossible for native wild flowers to grow.

Gray Squirrels

The gray squirrel was introduced to the United Kingdom from North America in the nineteenth century as a curiosity to add interest to parks. No one predicted how successful this species would be and how damaging it would be to the native red squirrel. Some evidence suggests that gray squirrels carry the parapox virus, which is harmless to them, but deadly to red squirrels. This puts red squirrels at a disadvantage whenever the species are in close proximity.

Since gray squirrels are larger, stronger, and more disease-resistant than reds, they were able to out-compete the reds. Gray squirrels prefer broadleaf woodlands. As a result, the red squirrels have retreated mainly to the coniferous forests of the north of England and Scotland—although a couple of isolated populations continue to exist in southern England and Wales. Today, there are an estimated 2.5 million gray squirrels in England and Wales, and fewer than 140,000 reds.

The Nutria: From Fur to Fear

The nutria is a large rodent. Weighing approximately 24 pounds (11 kg), it was imported to the United States from South America in the 1930s.

Nutria were farmed for their fur, which was used in the expanding fur trade. During the 1940s, the market for fur collapsed and with it the nutria farms.

CASE STUDY

MARSHLAND IN DANGER

Another unanticipated consequence of the introduction of nutria has been the loss of salt marsh across Chesapeake Bay in the eastern United States. Between 1970 and 2010, up to 6,900 acres (2,800 ha) of salt marsh were lost as a result of overfeeding by nutria. The nutria likes to eat the roots and tubers of marsh-growing plants, such as bulrushes. The roots act as a glue, holding together the sediment that makes up the fragile soil of the salt marshes. When the roots are removed, the sediment washes away easily, making it difficult for plants to regrow.

Alaska

Yukon
Territory

Northern
Territories

British
Columbia

Alberta

Saskatchewan

Manitoba

Ontario

Quebec

Newfoundland

Prince
Edward
Island

New
Brunswick

Nova
Scotia

Maine

Washington

Montana

North
Dakota

Minnesota

Vermont

New Hampshire

Oregon

Idaho

South
Dakota

Wisconsin

Michigan

New
York

Massachusetts

Rhode Island

Wyoming

Iowa

Pennsylvania

Connecticut

Nevada

Nebraska

Illinois

Indiana

Ohio

West
Virginia

New Jersey

Delaware

Utah

Colorado

Kansas

Missouri

Kentucky

Virginia

Maryland

California

Washington D.C.

Arizona

New
Mexico

Oklahoma

Arkansas

Tennessee

North Carolina

South Carolina

Texas

Louisiana

Mississippi

Alabama

Georgia

Florida

N

500 km

500 miles

Nutria population established due to
escape or release

Nutria range expansion

Nutria never established

Nutria no longer found

Source of nutria population unknown

No data available

This map shows how the nutria spread across
the United States, having escaped or been
released from farms in the southern states
and from Washington and Oregon.

Many farmers simply turned their nutria
loose. Nutria are more aggressive than
the native muskrat and reproduce rapidly.
In one isolated region of approximately
10,000 acres (4,000 ha) in Dorchester
County, Maryland, the nutria population has
increased from 150 in 1968 to approximately
50,000 today. As a result of this invasion,
muskrats have been forced out.

The Effects of Climate Change

The term climate change means an alteration to long-term global weather patterns. This could include a change in average global temperatures, as well as increased instances of drought, storms, and flooding. At the moment, Earth's climate is gradually becoming warmer, so climate change is often referred to as global warming. While some scientists doubt that human actions are responsible for climate change, the vast majority agree that we are contributing to changes in our planet's climate. This, in turn, has a major impact on the planet's animals and plants.

Adaptation

Animal and plant species are capable of adapting to changes in climate. Some do this gradually by physical adaptation. One example is the large ears of the fennec fox. These are a physical adaptation to the changing conditions in the Sahara where the fennec fox lives. The large ears fill with blood, which is then able to cool, thus dispersing excess heat from the fox's body. Thousands of years ago, as the Sahara became hotter, some ancestors of the fennec fox were born with larger ears. It was easier for these fox to survive in the new conditions. Over the years, the bigger-eared fox were more successful and mated with each other, leading to the birth of even bigger-eared foxes, which were even better suited to the climate.

Migration

Sometimes animals are able to adapt by migrating to areas where the climate is more suitable for them. Swallows, for example, spend the winter in the southern hemisphere, then migrate to the northern hemisphere in the summer. They travel great distances each year to find the warmest weather—rather like humans going on their vacations!

Dangers of Climate Change

But what happens when changes to the climate happen too fast for species to adapt to through evolution? What happens when species cannot leave their current range due to physical barriers, such as seas, mountain ranges, or human settlement? We may find that some species become

Each of these cows releases up to 53 gallons (200 L) of methane every day. Methane is more than 20 times more powerful than carbon dioxide as a greenhouse gas.

HUMAN CAUSES OF CLIMATE CHANGE

Humans have contributed to climate change mostly through emissions of carbon dioxide. This is a greenhouse gas, which means it is a type of gas that traps the sun's heat within Earth's atmosphere (like the glass walls of a greenhouse), helping to warm the planet. We create carbon dioxide by burning fossil fuels (coal, oil, and gas). Much of this carbon dioxide is absorbed by the planet's trees in a process called photosynthesis. But because we have cut down so many trees in the rain forests and other forested areas, less carbon dioxide is being absorbed. We also contribute to climate change by farming cattle on a vast scale. One cow emits up to 53 gallons (200 L) of methane per day. Methane is a powerful greenhouse gas. With an estimated 1.5 billion cattle on Earth today, this can make a significant impact.

endangered or even extinct as a result of climate change.

Polar Bears: Feeling the Heat

Polar bears live within the Arctic Circle, which encompasses parts of Alaska, northwest Canada, Greenland, some parts of Norway, and northern Russia. All of these lands surround the Arctic Ocean. The polar ice cap is at the center of the Arctic Ocean. This area extends 500 miles (800 km) south from the North Pole and is always frozen. The rest of the Arctic Ocean freezes only in the winter when the area of ice more than doubles. On this outer ring of pack ice, polar bears like to hunt during the winter months.

As global temperatures have risen over the last few decades, the area of pack ice has decreased. In 2005, the pack ice receded 200 miles (320 km) farther than it did in the 1970s. The ice is also much thinner with an average thickness of 6 feet (1.8 m) today, compared to 10 feet (3 m) in the 1950s. Average temperatures on the northern coast of Alaska are approximately 3.6°F (2°C) higher than they were in 1949.

Polar bears like to hunt on the edges of the pack ice, where it is thinner, to catch their favorite food—ringed and bearded seals. Using their excellent sense of smell, they find a seal's breathing hole in the ice. Then they crouch down nearby and wait. When the seal puts its head above water to breathe, the polar bear strikes. Polar bears need to eat only every four to five days, but finding sufficient food on the shrinking pack ice is becoming increasingly difficult.

The Big Swim

Polar bears also hunt on ice floes—areas of ice that have broken away from the pack ice and float on the sea. As the ice melts, the bears are forced to swim farther to get to new ice. In 1986, about 4 percent of all polar bears sighted were swimming. By 2005, this had increased to 20 percent. They are excellent swimmers, so a sea crossing of 18.6 miles (30 km) is not difficult. But increasingly, gaps between ice floes suitable for polar bears to hunt from are widening to 62 miles (100 km) or more. Swimming this length can leave the bears exhausted and vulnerable to hypothermia.

Signs of pressure on the polar bear include instances of cannibalism in which bears have eaten their own cubs. While this is not common, frequency has increased from one or two cases per year to at least eight.

FACTS and FIGURES

A BLEAK FUTURE

The IUCN Red List for 2010 lists polar bears as vulnerable. The IUCN expects polar bear populations to decline by more than 30 percent in the coming 45 years. Summer sea ice is expected to reduce by 50 to 100 percent by 2100. Polar bears are thought to be unable to adapt quickly enough to the changed conditions caused by continual climate change. It is likely they will have almost disappeared in the wild within 100 years.

Source: IUCN Red List, February 2010

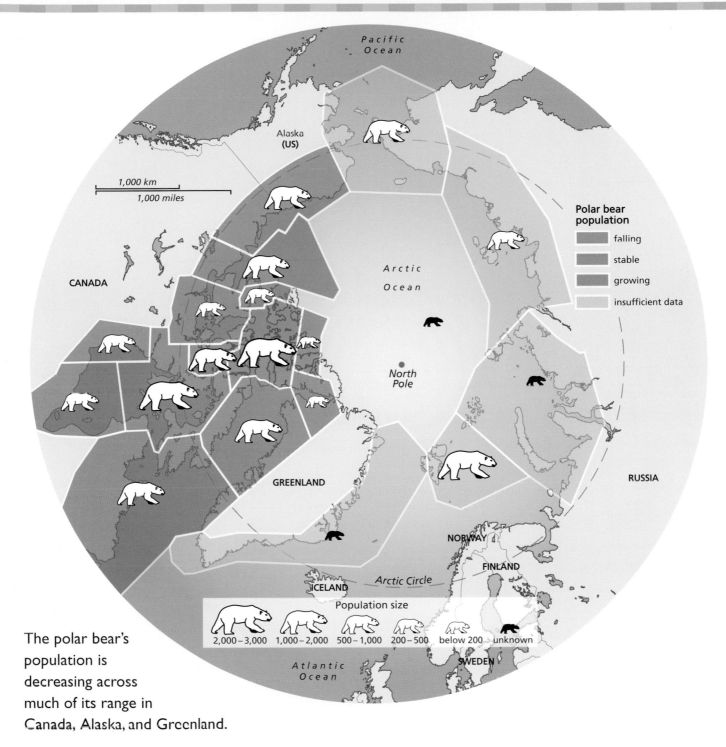

The polar bear's population is decreasing across much of its range in Canada, Alaska, and Greenland.

The Golden Toads

The golden toad once lived in significant numbers in Costa Rica's Monteverde Cloud Forest Reserve. The species was discovered by humans in 1966 and was endemic—that is, it could not be found anywhere else in the world.

In 1987, researchers counted several thousand golden toads, which had gathered to breed in pools. Just one year later, only 10 golden toads were found. In 1989, only one

Male golden toads have not been seen in the Monteverde Cloud Forest of Costa Rica since 1989, when a single male was found. They are now classified by the IUCN as extinct.

toad was seen. Since then, no golden toads have been seen and are now classified by the IUCN as extinct.

So what caused the sudden extinction of an entire species? The cloud forests, high up in the mountains, are often shrouded in mist, which gives them their name and provides the moisture the forest needs during the January to April dry season. Since the 1970s, the frequency of the mists has declined significantly as a result of the warming of the oceans and the atmosphere.

El Niño is a climate pattern that occurs about every five years in the tropical Pacific region and causes unusually warm waters on the South American coast. An El Niño event in 1988–89 made the climate in Costa Rica particularly warm and dry—conditions that the golden toad may not have been able to survive. The warm conditions may also have helped chytrid, a fungal disease, to flourish. Chytrid has been responsible for wiping out many amphibian populations and may have contributed to the extinction of the golden toad.

The Snowdon Lily: Clinging to Survival

The Snowdon lily is a remnant of the last ice age. It thrives on the high, rocky crags of Snowdon in North Wales, where it is well suited to the cold, harsh conditions. However, climate scientists predict that Snowdon may lose its snowcap altogether by 2020 if the climate continues to get warmer at its current rate. This may make the Snowdon lily's survival on the mountain impossible. With warmer temperatures higher up the mountain, other plants will soon start to spread and choke out the last six colonies of Snowdon lilies on the mountain. Hopefully, colonies of the lilies in the Alps and Rocky Mountains will ensure the continuation of the species.

With a Welsh population of fewer than 100 bulbs, the Snowdon lily may become the first plant to become extinct in the British Isles as a result of global warming.

Oceans in Danger

Humans have eaten fish for thousands of years. For most of that time, humans either were not numerous enough or lacked the technology to threaten the vast numbers of marine animals in the world's seas and oceans. However, as the human population has expanded, and demand has increased, we have developed ways of catching fish in ever greater numbers. Now there is a real danger that we will wipe out many species.

Atlantic Cod

The Atlantic cod was added to a list of endangered species by WWF in 2000. In 2010, Greenpeace International added the Atlantic cod to its Seafood Red List. This is a list of fish commonly sold in supermarkets around the world that have a very high risk of being sourced from unsustainable fisheries. That is, they have been caught in areas of the ocean that have been overfished. In these areas, the fish are being caught in such quantities that they can no longer replace their numbers through breeding, and the population declines.

Arguments About Quotas

Countries that fish for Atlantic cod, including the United Kingdom, the United States, and Canada, have imposed quotas on their fishermen by limiting the amount of fish they are allowed to catch each year. It is debatable whether these quotas are low enough to ensure the cod's survival. More distressingly, once fishermen reach their annual quota for a particular species, they must throw back any more fish of that species they catch during the rest of the year. In this way, thousands of tons of fish are caught and, once dead, are wastefully thrown back into the sea.

The fishermen argue that they have to make a living. Many urge that quotas be increased. However, if the quotas are raised, it reduces the chances that enough cod is left in the sea to replenish stocks for the following year. By overfishing, the fishermen could ultimately bring about the end of their industry by driving species, such as cod, to extinction.

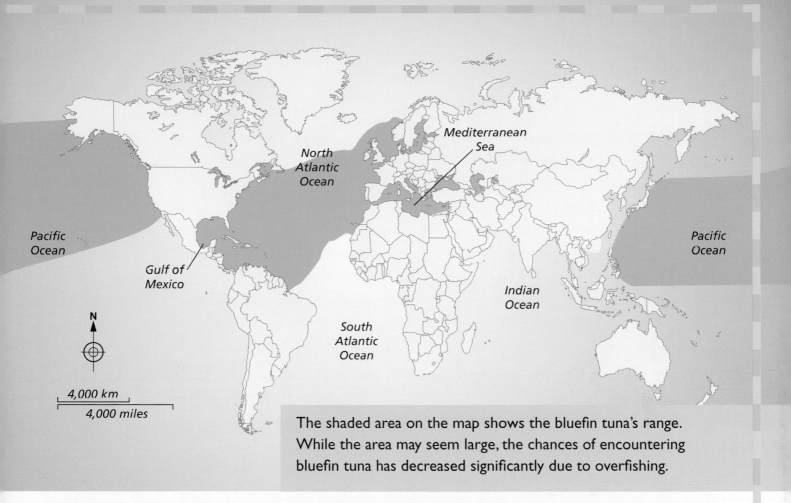

North
Atlantic
Ocean

Mediterranean
Sea

Pacific
Ocean

Pacific
Ocean

Gulf of
Mexico

Indian
Ocean

South
Atlantic
Ocean

N

4,000 km
4,000 miles

The shaded area on the map shows the bluefin tuna's range.
While the area may seem large, the chances of encountering
bluefin tuna has decreased significantly due to overfishing.

CASE STUDY

BLUEFIN TUNA

Bluefin tuna can grow to 10 feet (3 m) in length and weigh up to 1,433 pounds (650 kg). It is used extensively for Japanese sushi, and 75 percent of all bluefin tuna is eaten in Japan. The fish has become very valuable with a single fish selling for more than $396,000 in Japan in January 2011.

There are three separate bluefin tuna populations: two in the Atlantic Ocean and one, the southern bluefin tuna, in the Indian and Pacific oceans. Stocks of all three have declined very rapidly in recent decades. Although the

IUCN does not have up-to-date information on the bluefin tuna, it classifies the Eastern Atlantic stock as endangered, the Western Atlantic stock as critically endangered, and the southern bluefin tuna also as critically endangered.

Conservationists argue that urgent action is required to limit the fishing of this species, or there is a real danger that it will not recover. In March 2010, at a meeting of the Convention on International Trade in Endangered Species (CITES) (see page 38), Monaco attempted to ban international trade in Atlantic bluefin tuna, but this proposal was rejected.

Whaling

Whales have been hunted for centuries. Archaeological evidence from the North Atlantic shows that the Inuit were killing whales as early as 3000 BC. They did so to feed their families, and a single whale would last a long time. This kind of hunting posed no threat to the whale population.

Industrial Whaling

By the nineteenth century, a whaling industry had built up around Antarctica, where whales were plentiful. Many different whales migrated there during the southern hemisphere's summer to feed on the immense swarms of krill that gathered around the Antarctic coast. Many different products were made from whale parts. Whale oils were regarded as among the purest in the world and were used in lighting and as lubricants for delicate machinery. Baleen was also highly prized. This is the filtering structure in the mouths of most species of whale, which they use to sieve small animals such as krill from large mouthfuls of water. Baleen was used to create items such as carriage springs, fishing rods, and hoops for ladies' skirts.

In 1868, Svend Foyn, a Norwegian, invented the exploding harpoon. This large spear-like weapon was fired from a cannon into the body of a whale. The harpoon was attached by a rope to the ship from which it was fired. Once inside the whale's body, the harpoon exploded, killing the whale. As faster, steam-powered ships were developed, keeping up with whales was no longer a problem, and with the exploding harpoon, killing them became easier. Not surprisingly, many whale species were driven close to extinction by the whaling industry.

Blue Whale

The population of blue whales dropped from between 200,000 and 300,000 in the early nineteenth century to just 1,000–2,000 by 1966, when the International Whaling Commission (IWC) imposed a worldwide ban on hunting this species. The largest examples caught were 108 feet (33 m) long and weighed 195 tons (177 t), making the blue whale the largest animal ever known to have existed. In 2010, the WWF estimated the blue whale population in the Southern Ocean at 2,300. Blue whales are still regarded by the IUCN as endangered. It takes 5 to 15 years for a blue whale to reach sexual maturity, and whales give birth only every two to three years. It will take a very long time for their numbers to recover.

International Whaling Ban

Since 1986, there has been a ban on all commercial whaling. In 1994, the IWC created the Southern Ocean Whale Sanctuary, making all whaling illegal in the Southern Ocean.

However, since the ban was imposed, Japanese whalers have killed more than

9,000 whales for "scientific research" purposes. The meat from the whales is then sold as food in Japan. According to the whalers, the main reason for this research is to investigate the health and population size of whale species to provide evidence that their populations have recovered sufficiently for whale hunting to begin again, albeit with strict limits on catch sizes. In 2010, the IWC came under renewed pressure from Japan, Norway, and Iceland—the three leading whaling nations—to lift the ban on whaling. It may only be a matter of time before commercial whaling is resumed.

The blue whale is the world's largest animal—of this or any other time in Earth's history. Its heart weighs about 1,325 pounds (600 kg) and its tongue weighs up to 3 tons (2.7 t).

PERSPECTIVES

NOT THE TIME TO END THE BAN

In 2010, when whales face even more threats than ever before—including toxic pollution, climate change, loss of habitat, ship strikes, and oil and gas exploration—how could anyone believe it's safe to let whalers off their leash?

Excerpt from a letter to the IWC, written by actor Pierce Brosnan on behalf of the Humane Society of the United States

Antarctic Krill—an Endangered Species?

Krill are tiny, shrimp-like crustaceans that live in all of the world's oceans. Antarctic krill live in the Southern Ocean and, at 2 inches (5 cm) long, are the largest of all krill species. They feed on phytoplankton (microscopic plants that live in the sea), which are abundant in the Antarctic.

The world's population of Antarctic krill is estimated to weigh more than the weight of the world's population of people. How can they possibly be under threat? Still, their numbers have declined by up to 80 percent since the 1970s, according to National Geographic.

Scientists believe that the main cause of this decline is climate change. Average temperatures in the Antarctic have increased by 4.5°F (2.5°C) in the last 50 years. There is now less sea ice and fewer places where ice algae, on which the Antarctic krill feed, can grow. Less pack ice also means fewer cave-like structures in the ice, which krill need for shelter in the early stages of their development.

The decline in the krill population is bad news for the Antarctic ecosystem as a whole. Krill provides food for many larger creatures, including baleen whales, squids, penguins, and crabeater seals. The Antarctic krill is the foundation for life in the Southern Ocean. If they disappear, then the species above them in the food pyramid will also tumble and fall.

Coral

Coral reefs are unique underwater ecosystems that are home to a quarter of all the world's known marine life. Corals are made up of polyps, tiny living creatures that join together to form colonies. The polyps' skeletons are made of white calcium carbonate, yet corals are very colorful and can be red, orange, yellow, green, pink, blue, and purple. Their color comes from colonies of tiny, single-celled plants called zooxanthellae. Corals feed off the zooxanthellae, obtaining 90 percent of their energy from them. In return, they give the zooxanthellae the protection, shelter, nutrients, and carbon dioxide they need to survive. This is called a symbiotic relationship because both sides benefit.

Corals are sensitive to increases in temperature. Higher water temperatures and greater light intensity, even for periods of just eight weeks, can kill the zooxanthellae, causing the coral to starve. The coral becomes bleached—a white, lifeless skeleton.

Australia's Great Barrier Reef is a vast coral reef. More than 1,430 miles (2,300 km) in length, it is the world's largest living structure. It is home to 400 species of coral, 1,500 species of fish, 30 species of whale and dolphin, and 6 species of turtle. In 1998 and 2002, the Great Barrier Reef experienced bleaching events. The first killed 42 percent and the second killed 54 percent of its coral. Most areas have since recovered from these

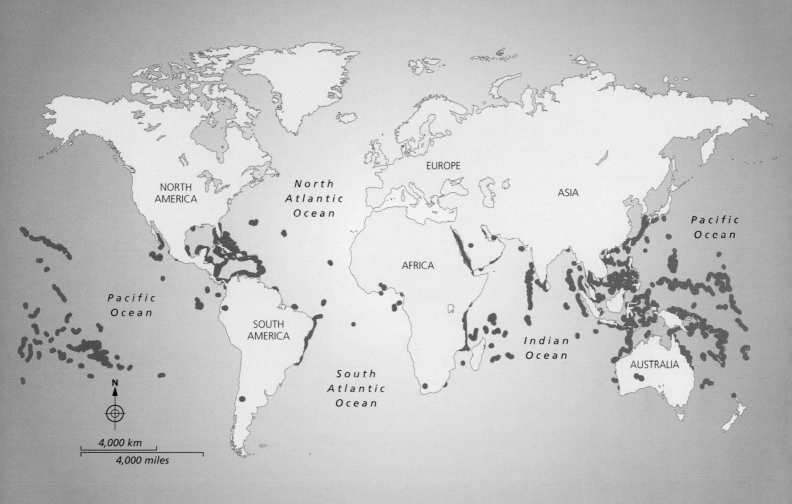

This map shows the location of the world's coral reefs. All are located in tropical waters. Seventy percent of coral reefs could be destroyed by 2050 if global temperatures continue to increase at current rates.

events. However, based on conservative estimates for climate change provided by the Intergovernmental Panel on Climate Change (IPCC), by 2100 coral around the world will suffer regular bleaching events in the summer.

PERSPECTIVES

REEFS IN DANGER

Coral reefs are incredibly important to ocean health ... but if we don't act, we could lose 70 percent of reefs worldwide by the middle of the century.

Stephanie Wear, the Nature Conservancy's coral expert, from *Time* magazine, August 29, 2010

Solutions

The previous chapters have shown that, as a species, humans have threatened or wiped out other species. This has occurred through deliberate acts, such as hunting or overfishing, or as a byproduct of our activities, such as pollution or deforestation. Is it all bad news? Are humans the ultimate destroyers of life on Earth? Thankfully, the news is not all bad. In fact, many people have devoted their lives to preserving the species that share the planet. And there are those who are working to reduce the impacts that our activities have on other species around the globe.

CITES

The Convention on International Trade in Endangered Species of Wild Fauna and Flora (known as CITES) is an international agreement between governments and came into force in 1975. It currently offers varying degrees of protection to approximately 33,000 animal and plant species. The purpose of CITES is to prevent countries from buying and selling goods that have originated from endangered species. These include elephant ivory and tiger parts. So far, only one species under CITES' protection has become extinct in the wild. This is the Spix's macaw. However, its numbers were so low before CITES came into force that most likely its demise was inevitable.

Reserves: A Hope for Survival?

Game reserves, if they are well policed, provide a real refuge for endangered species to live their lives free from the threat of hunters and loggers. In areas where their habitat is protected and where hunting is banned, endangered species stand a much better chance of survival. Generally, where they are not under pressure, species are likely to breed more successfully.

Zoos: Good or Bad?

Not everyone agrees that zoos should exist. The idea of keeping animals in captivity for public entertainment seems cruel and unnecessary. This was certainly a justifiable criticism of zoos in the past. However, many zoos today play a vital role in the survival

A sight you're not likely to see in the wild: the Spix's macaw is now thought to be extinct in its rain forest home and lives only as a captive species.

of extremely rare species. In many cases, the species being looked after in the world's zoos are dying out in the wild. Zoos also help to raise public awareness about the plight of endangered species and encourage more people to get involved in conservation.

Captive Breeding

Zoos can also offer captive breeding programs, helping threatened species to breed in safety. The ultimate purpose

CASE STUDY

THE SPIX'S MACAW

The last known Spix's macaw in the wild (a male) disappeared from its Brazilian rain forest home in 2000. The Spix's macaw suffered from the loss of its habitat and was also targeted by the exotic pet trade. This species, which was discovered just 150 years ago, now survives only in captivity, and there are not many. In 2000, there were thought to be only 54 captive Spix's macaws still living.

of most captive breeding programs is to reintroduce endangered species to their natural habitats once they exist in sufficient numbers. Captive breeding programs need to address a number of issues:

- There needs to be a sufficiently broad gene pool to prevent inbreeding. That is, zoos must ensure that related animals do not breed with each other as it causes weaker offspring. Zoos across the world often cooperate with each other on captive breeding programs to ensure the gene pool is sufficiently broad.

- If a species is threatened by habitat destruction, and the habitat destruction continues, there may be nowhere left in the wild where the species can be reintroduced. Some argue that funds used for captive breeding programs would be better spent helping to preserve species in their natural habitat.

- Captive-bred animals need to be nurtured in an environment as similar to their natural habitat as possible. Otherwise, they are likely to be much less capable of hunting, foraging, finding shelter, and avoiding predators when reintroduced to the wild.

A Success Story: The Golden Lion Tamarin

The golden lion tamarin of the Brazilian rain forest was a species in severe decline. By 1993, there were just 272 in the wild and were classified as "critically endangered" on the IUCN Red List. An international captive breeding program, together with better habitat protection, has helped increase the population to more than 1,000 in the wild, and 500 in captivity by 2010. One-third of the wild population is made up of reintroduced animals. The golden lion tamarin's status was downgraded to endangered in 2003.

Holidays on the Wild Side

People's awareness of endangered species has grown over recent decades. Many have become interested in seeing species in their original habitats—normally inaccessible and almost untouched areas of the planet. This has given rise to a new trend known as ecological tourism, or ecotourism, which can help endangered species survive. If the local population can be convinced that they can make more money by allowing people to come and look at the endangered species than they can by hunting those species or destroying their habitats, they are more likely to want to preserve them.

Some of the profits from ecotourism are fed directly into conservation work, benefiting the very species that the tourists have come to see. In many countries, ecotourism is now big business. If you are tempted to take a trip into the wilderness, it is important to check that the tour will not cause further damage to the area you want to visit.

The golden lion tamarin has been brought back from the brink of extinction through good protection in the wild and successful captive breeding and reintroduction programs.

FACTS and FIGURES

WHALE WATCHING

Whale watching is an activity that many ecotourists enjoy. In 2009, whale watching brought in $2.1 billion worldwide and employed some 13,000 people. And its popularity is set to grow. According to forecasts, the industry could soon be worth up to $2.5 billion and employ 19,000 people.

Source: A. M. Cisneros Montemayor, U. R. Sumaila, K. Kaschner, and D. Pauly, University of British Colombia, 2010

You Can Help Too!

As discussed earlier, climate change creates problems for many species. Think about how you can reduce your impact on the planet every day. Do you really need to take the car? Could you walk, cycle, or take public transportation instead?

You can support conservation projects. Many charities help to preserve the endangered species of the world. Some, like WWF, deal with various environmental problems. Others, like the Orangutan Foundation, specialize in the preservation of a particular species. Search the web to determine which organizations work to support a particular species that interests you.

You can provide support by raising funds for the organizations concerned. This helps pay for their conservation and awareness-raising work. Some offer the opportunity to "adopt an animal." Any money you raise will help support a particular animal that the organization looks after in the wild. They usually provide regular updates on the individual animal's progress.

In Conclusion

Thousands of species are under threat in the world today. It is vital that young people learn about their plight so that the movement to preserve and protect them continues into the future. We need to learn how to treat our world in a way that does less damage. If we take too much from our planet, we may find one day that we have become the next endangered species!

Tourists experience a close encounter with a polar bear. In the future, ecotourism may generate the income needed to protect the species that tourists are paying to see.

Glossary

adaptation A change in structure, function, or behavior by which a species or individual improves its chance of survival in a specific environment.

background extinction rate The standard rate of extinction in Earth's geological and biological history before humans became a major cause of extinctions.

bioaccumulation The accumulation of a substance, such as a toxic chemical, in the tissues of a living organism.

climate The general or average weather conditions of a certain region, including temperature, rainfall, and wind.

conservation-reliant species Endangered or threatened species that require continuing human intervention to survive.

DDT Dichlorodiphenyltrichloroethane—a powerful insecticide that can cause hormonal changes, such as decreased fertility and reproductive problems, to top predators.

deforestation The cutting down and removal of all or most of the trees in a forested area.

ecosystem A community of interacting organisms and their physical environment.

ecotourism Tourism to exotic, often threatened, natural environments to support conservation efforts and observe wildlife.

endangered species A species, whose numbers are so small, that it is at risk of extinction.

endemic Native to or confined to a certain region.

extinct in the wild A species in which the only known living members are in captivity.

extinction Complete destruction or annihilation.

food chain A series of organisms, each dependent on the next as a source of food.

fossil fuel A natural fuel, such as coal, oil, or gas, formed in the geological past from the remains of living organisms.

fossil record Fossils preserved in layers of rocks that scientists can study.

glacier A slowly moving mass of ice.

greenhouse gas Any of the atmospheric gases, such as carbon dioxide and methane, that contribute to global warming.

habitat The environment in which an animal or plant normally lives or grows.

hides Skins obtained from animals for human use.

ice age A period in Earth's history when polar and mountain ice sheets spread across large parts of Earth's surface. The most recent ice age ended about 10,000 years ago.

ice floe A mass or sheet of floating ice.

IUCN The International Union for the Conservation of Nature and Natural Resources.

ivory A substance that forms the bulk of the teeth and tusks of animals such as elephants.

krill Small crustaceans that exist in the ocean in huge numbers. They are the main food of baleen whales.

metabolize The process in which food is changed to energy to maintain life.

near threatened A conservation status assigned to species that may be threatened with extinction in the near future.

phytoplankton Minute, free-floating aquatic plants.

poaching Illegal hunting, fishing, or harvesting of wild plants or animals.

pollution Contamination of the environment with harmful substances.

Red List The world's most comprehensive inventory of the global conservation status of plant and animal species. The Red List is compiled by the IUCN.

species A group of living organisms consisting of similar individuals that are capable of interbreeding.

Further Information

Books

The Atlas of Endangered Species (third edition) by Richard Mackay (Earthscan, 2008)

Endangered Planet by David Burnie (Kingfisher Books, 2004)

Animals on the Edge: Science Races to Save Species Threatened with Extinction by Sandy Pobst (National Geographic, 2008)

100 Things You Should Know About Endangered Animals by Steve Parker (Miles Kelly, 2009)

What If We Do Nothing? Endangered Species by Sean Sheehan (Gareth Stevens Publishing, 2009)

Web Sites

http://animals.howstuffworks.com/endangered-species
This Discovery web site discusses the endangered cheetah, the importance of the diminishing bee population, and why frogs and other amphibians are facing extinction.

http://animals.nationalgeographic.com/animals/conservation/
This National Geographic site has images and information regarding animals, such as gorillas, big cats, and elephants, that are part of conservation projects.

www.arkive.org/
Amazing videos of endangered species to view online plus great facts.

www.iucnredlist.org
Information on the state of the world's endangered species.

www.wwf.org.uk
Information on the state of the world's endangered species and the work that the World Wildlife Fund carries out.

Index